Mata Hari's Lost Words

Second Edition

John Oughton

NeoPoiesisPress.com

NeoPoiesis Press, LLC

2775 Harbor Ave SW, Suite D, Seattle, WA
Info@NeoPoiesisPress.com
NeoPoiesisPress.com

John Oughton – Mata Hari's Lost Words
ISBN 978-0-9975021-5-2 (paperback: alk. paper)

    1. Poetry. I. Oughton, John. II. Mata Hari's Lost Words.

Library of Congress Control Number: 2016961645

Second Edition

Design, art direction & typography: Milo Duffin and Stephen Roxborough

Printed in the United States of America

One of me is standing in the waves, an ocean bather,
or I am naked with a plate of devils at my hip.
                                                Grace
to be born and live as variously as possible. The conception
of the masque barely suggests the sordid identifications.

— Frank O'Hara *"In Memory of My Feelings"*

Contents

Preface

This book was first published in 1988, the year my daughter was born. It resulted from a long obsession with Mata Hari and the many stories about her. At the time, the Web resources we now take for granted were science fiction, so my research involved libraries and books.

Writing this sequence was a major challenge for me as a poet. My previous books had been inspired by my own experiences. To write this one, I had to find a new and distinct voice, imagine myself as a different gender, and convey the flavor of life in the Belle Époque before WWI. It was a stretch and, I hope, resulted in some of the best poetry I have yet written. My sister Libby Oughton owned Ragweed Press in Charlottetown, PEI, and offered to publish the book. The press no longer exists, and the book has long been out of print. Quotations from Mata Hari's own writing are placed between sections of this edition

Now that the deadline for release of Mata Hari's trial documents and memoirs is near, it seems appropriate to issue a new and slightly expanded edition. One poem has been added (*Interview with a Journalist*) and I have made minor revisions to the others. I have added material to the introduction to reflect some recent news about the world's most famous female spy.

I thank: Kath MacLean for urging me to create a new edition; Dale Winslow and her press NeoPoiesis for publishing it; and horror writer Sephira Giron for retyping the manuscript from a copy of the original book.

Introduction

The Myth

Sometime in 2017, hundred-year-old secrets will be uncovered. They detail the trial and execution of one of the most notorious and enigmatic women ever. Who was she? And what exactly was she guilty of?

The life of Margaretha Gertruuida Zelle, also known as Mata Hari, inspired this sequence of poems. Like Marilyn Monroe's, her legend grew after she died in middle age. Both were more complex than their popular images suggest: Mata Hari was an independent, accomplished woman whose spying was her least successful venture. Today, the name "Mata Hari" connotes a glamorous, man-destroying woman spy, a curvier James Bond with eye make-up. In fact, Mata Hari was trapped and destroyed by men.

Certain people inspire myths because we need them as archetypes. If Monroe fulfilled a psychic need for a dumb, blonde, child-woman sex goddess, Mata Hari minted the other side of the coin: the dark, seductive succubus who kills with a kiss. She was the apotheosis of the femme fatale. This image has a long history; Lilith, Circe, Medusa, Salomé, and Cleopatra, are exemplars. The femme fatale was especially common in nineteenth-century European culture, turning up in Keats' *"La Belle Dame Sans Merci,"* and countless paintings and drawings of the Sphinx, Medea, Salomé, vampires and bat-women. Artists like Beardsley, Klimt, Munch and Von Stuck were as drawn to her as kitsch artists are to sad clowns. *Femme Fatale: Images of Evil and Fascinating Women* by Patrick Bode gives a good visual and verbal summary.

It is apparently common for twentieth-century politicians and generals to play out masochistic fantasies when alone with their mistresses or prostitutes. A century ago, women did not have the vote in most nations; perhaps the great social power men then had over women inspired a similar inversion in fantasy, giving cruel, omnipotent she-devils some force.

The most memorable products of this male artistic fixation are the opera *Salomé* (music by Richard Strauss, libretto based on Oscar Wilde's *Salomé*) in which the heroine kisses the severed head of the prophet Iokannon, and Edvard Munch's paintings, haunted by women who tempt the viewer to madness as well as death. Swinburne summed up the archetype in a few lines:

> You are crueller, you that we love,
> than hatred, hunger, or death;
> You have eyes and breasts like a dove,
> And you kill men's hearts with a breath.

Although the power of the femme fatale over male imagination began to fade by 1900, traces are still evident in the twentieth century. In movies alone, Theda Bara, Marlene Dietrich, Barbara Stanwyck, Rita Hayworth, and Jane Russell have all played femme fatale roles. More recent is Glenn Close in the appropriately titled *Fatal Attraction*.

Mata Hari's height (5'10" in a time when most women were closer to 5'), dark colouring, solemn expression and undeniable powers of seduction made her heiress to the tradition. Although it no doubt added to her power as a courtesan, the archetype contributed to her execution. A military jury would have been less likely to condemn her to death on such circumstantial evidence had she been short, fair and innocent-looking.

The fact that larger psychological forces were at work is underlined by the French authorities' handling of her case. Unsatisfied with merely executing her, they auctioned off her belongings, refused to deliver her last letter to her daughter, sent her remains to a medical school for dissection, and locked up her memoirs in French military archives until 2017. This was presumably because of the military and political figures implicated in them. We may never completely know her side of the story. Such obliteration suggests that Mata Hari's misfortune was to represent more than a spy.

She has had a grip on my own imagination, for reasons I don't fully understand. These poems attempt to evoke and exorcise that obsession, and pay tribute to a remarkable woman.

The Facts

Mata Hari was expert at spinning tales about herself. Many of her early biographers (including her father, who made a few guilders from a cobbled-together "Life of") were no more scrupulous with the facts. Among the most colourful versions of her life is the Greta Garbo movie. At least Garbo was tall, unlike Jeanne Moreau, another cinematic Mata Hari.

The facts used in these poems are largely drawn from *Eye of Dawn* by Erika Ostrovsky, the most readable and objective of the biographies. The more recent *Mata Hari: The True Story* by Russell Warren Howe draws on research into excerpts from the secret military archives, but is marred by the author's refusal to believe she could have been much of a dancer or beauty.

In 1876, Mata Hari was born Margaretha Gertruuida Zelle in Frisia, Holland's northernmost region. She was the youngest child of Adam Zelle, a local hat merchant whose initial affluence was soon followed by bankruptcy. She became a dark, slender woman, with remarkable black eyes.

At nineteen, she met Rudolph MacLeod through a "Companions Wanted" ad a friend had placed for him as a joke. He was twenty years older and an officer in the Dutch colonial army. They soon married, a daughter already on the way, and then were posted to Java. There a son was born, who died, some thought poisoned by a native.

The couple fought; he was often drunk and abusive. After his retirement, they returned to Europe and divorced. She began a career as an exotic dancer in Paris, passing herself off as an Indian temple dancer of royal blood. The religious connection allowed European reviewers and audiences to treat her highly erotic performances as sacred art from the mysterious East.

In fact, however tenuous the relationship of her dancing to the real thing, she did prepare the way for the Javanese dancers and Indian orchestras who toured Europe after her. Her stage name, Mata Hari, meant Eye of Dawn (morning sun) in Javanese. At her peak, she rivalled Isadora Duncan in popularity.

As her dancing career waned, she became Europe's leading courtesan, sought by men of power and wealth everywhere. The courtesans of the time — Mata Hari, La Belle Otero, Cora Pearl, Cléo de la Mérode and others — might be compared to today's Kardashian sisters and more scandalous movie stars. Unlike call girls, they revelled in publicity. Their fashions, romances and crises fuelled racy conversation and tabloid gossip columns. The most successful spent their peak years in a froth of champagne, banquets, costume balls and assignations, commanding fees high enough to turn down men they didn't like. Many of their clients were noblemen (King Léopold of Belgium, the Prince of Wales, the Czar), politicians and millionaires.

On the day World War One began, Mata Hari drove through the festive streets of Berlin with the chief of police. Since Holland was neutral, she was able to travel to countries on both sides of the war. This, combined with her many influential lovers and command of five languages, may have inspired the Germans to recruit her as a spy. There could hardly have been a worse choice for undercover work; unlike John le Carré's colourless Smiley, she was recognized throughout Europe. She may have trained at a German spy school run by Elizabeth Schragmüller, the notorious "Fraulein Doktor." It remains unclear whether Mata Hari did spying of real benefit either to the Germans or the French, for whom she offered to work during interrogation. She did fall in love with a young Russian airman, Vadim de Masloff, only serving to increase French suspicion of her. Mata Hari said ruefully that she could never resist a man in uniform. Probably both sides suspected her of being a double agent and decided she was expendable.

In 1917, she was trapped in Paris after a telegram was decoded that mentioned a payment to her, sent by the Germans in a cypher they knew the French could break. French morale was low. War seemed endless after three years of trench fighting and massive casualties, and Paris had endured an unusually cold winter. Something was needed to lift spirits: what better than a public trial of a notorious foreign woman?

She insisted in her trial that the German payment was for her sexual services. By then, months spent in a dank prison on a starchy diet had eroded her looks. It was alleged that her actions led to the death of 50,000 Allied soldiers. The comment after the war by one of her prosecutors that she was "a mediocre spy" (Fraulein Doktor called her a "dud") is probably more accurate. Although the Pope interceded for clemency on her behalf, the Dutch royal family refused to join him. After refusing a blindfold, she was executed in October 1917 by a squad of Zouaves.

Mata Hari was a woman of many talents who made her own way in a male-dominated world. It is a sad irony that she is now known only for her most dubious accomplishment. In the end, not only was the femme fatale image fatal to her, it also subsumed her.

It has made her an enduring source of inspiration though, with more than half a dozen biographies, several movies, at least three musicals, a novel, allusions in pop culture, and even "the fictional Indy's first sexual encounter in *The Adventures of Young Indiana Jones* episode *"Demons of Deception"* according to Wikipedia, which is never wrong.

The Legend Continues

Mata Hari's image continues to fascinate others, too. In 2001, lawyer Thibault de Montbrial asked the French Ministry of Justice to review her case. He was acting on behalf of a Dutch foundation, and quoted evidence found by Leon Schirmann, who wrote *The Mata Hari Affair*. Among other things, he stated that files declassified by British intelligence in 1999 revealed their agents had found no proof that she was a spy. De Montbrial's request was denied, partly because such requests had to come from a member of her family, and Mata Heari's daughter had died childless.

Bizarrely, another item appeared in 21st century news: "When no one claimed Mata Hari's corpse, it was donated to the Museum of Anatomy in Paris. Her body was dissected and her head removed and preserved in wax. Mata Hari's head became part of the museum's display of infamous criminals that were executed in the 18th, 19th, and 20th centuries. When the French Minister of Education threated to close the museum in 2000, the museum director decided to give the minister an inventory of the museum's collections. However, when he reviewed the list, he found that Mata Hari's head was missing. Officials at the Museum of Anatomy don't know when the head was taken or by who[m] (Hoffman 2000)." The source is StrangeRemains.com.

In 2007, a new biography appeared, by American historian Pat Shipman: *Femme Fatal: Love, Lies and the Unknown Life of Mata Hari*. It is based on any more declassified documents and looks in detail at the ramifications of Mata Hari's brief and tempestuous marriage to MacLeod, and in particular at the strong possibility that he infected her with syphilis, which was then passed on to their children. Shipman makes the argument that the couple's son died not from poison administered by a cast-off Javanese mistress, but rather the effects of the mercury treatment prescribed for him.

I am a woman who enjoys herself very much; sometimes I lose, sometimes I win.

The Goat-Cart

A child lives in a kaleidoscope.
Each turn of the planet
juggles known faces, shards of
colour in new combinations.
The first memory I have
of standing apart from tumbling shards:
my sixth birthday and I'm the windfall
apple of my father's eye.
Plump and formal, puffing a cigar
he might buy me the world
but this year settles on two prancing goats
and the tiny cart with me
as queen, goddess, charioteer
urging them on.
No other father in Leeuwarden so extravagant,
no other mother would let her daughter drive.
The town snoozes in midday sun.
My goats have eyes as opaque as Satan's.

My steeds prance along dusty streets.
A man curses as I almost run him down,
two little girls playing hopscotch
freeze and stare at me in fear.
I allow this rush of speed
to make me an icon, figurehead
who does not move
though my long dark hair flails the wind.

What this memory gives me:
knowing I can ignore my fear,
plunge into speed as if it were all I wanted
and all anyone will see of me:
the shining eyes,
the recklessness.

As a woman, dancing, I use the delicacy
of sharp hooves racing over cobblestones,
as the world rushes toward me I learn to stand
unmoved.

Our Father

Adam Zelle's shop sold the best hats
but the neighbours who bought
whispered that he put on airs
"The Baron," they'd jeer

Our big house and my silk dresses
silenced them then
My brothers and I called him Old A to Z
Papa was tree-high in his top hat
when he carried me on his shoulders

Something went wrong: money
ebbed away
Papa kept his top hat and scorn
while workmen carted off the oak wardrobe
my silk dresses inside
Then he tipped his hat
stepped beyond our family portrait's frame
We were another bad business decision
He had done his best. Good-bye
Abandoned us to the narrow charity
of cousins and aunts

I still keep two rules
as his legacy
No one can cart your pride away
Always leave before
you are left

After Mother's Funeral

I play this piano
to atone for her death
my mother mourned
only by her family
(no one else bothered to attend)
our pride broken in public
now privately interred

my fingers find between the white keys —
skull teeth, ivory grave fence —
the black stone notes that end
broken

I play nothing, and jam down the sustain pedal
as the piano hums its own threnody

the perennial favourite
unfinished sonata of the newly-alone
child whose mother has gone into
a dark cleft spaded in the earth
her only faithful suitor, death

(ashes to ashes, dust to dust
only truth in that lie of
a funeral service)

I assemble the triad
my father's pride, disgrace
abandoning of us, shade it with
the minor of losing part of myself

my right hand gathers grief and
shards it into the future

my left grasps my mother's pain
and roots it in earth

This piano is the silence my mother
becomes
the silence my fingers ripple and still
an instrument of the dead:
ivory stripped from elephants
wood cloven from trees

Three final notes
launch her funeral barge

I swear when I die no one will forget me
so easily. I play the piano
to obliterate all this —
then let the lid slam down on my hands.

I was not content at home…
I wanted to live like a colourful butterfly
in the sun.

Rendezvous at the Rijksmuseum: I

Newspaper advertisement: "Officer on home leave
from Dutch East Indies would like to meet girl
of pleasant character. Object matrimony."

The officer is 38, veteran of colonial wars
stained by the Java sun
heir to the honour of the Mac Leods

I am 18, an orphan, bored
Who cares what matrimony means
if it gets me out of here?

We arrange to meet
March 30, 1895 in
the Military, Naval and Colonial Collection
First I must pass under the caryatids
bored marble women who bear the roof
for this heap of Dutch Renaissance stone
Carved at their feet
are Wisdom, Justice, Beauty, Truth
I have beauty, the other virtues can wait

All this technique seems another excuse
making me wait for life to begin
Seize it now, I say
When I flow through a room of nudes
every man looks at me

My musical walk smokes mementoes off the walls
a barrel chest of medals flexes his mustache at me
I flirt and he inflates
I wink at the caryatids
Their eyes are blank
and can't see into marriage either

Among the battleaxes, banners and daggers
we recognize possibility
and pass through the Rijksmuseum walls
into space

This man can get me out of here
After that we'll see

In six days he proposes: yes
In three months we're married
Six months later, I give birth
by May we board the Java steamer

Child with(in) Woman

Full circle
circle full-
filled.

THIS is what my
body means now
this making full
encircling.

My tall curving form
hipbones holding
bowl of belly
was the visible moon.

Inside waited my child
once nameless, unknown

but now fills me so
that we are one curve, one globe
the woman in the moon.

Rounding to full
are my breasts now
an answering completion
above this completion in me.

Husband or hopeful lovers have
no place here. Men are far
below us, lost and cursing
their telescopes and charts.

Among lunar craters and crags
we walk on the Mare Tranquillitatas.
Child and I form a bowl
filled with silver dust.

Rendezvous at the Rijksmuseum: II

Rudolph, do you remember how we met?
I answered your ad and we arranged
to meet in the Rijksmuseum. Sshh —
I know exactly what you thought.
No, let me finish this —
then I'll come to bed.

"I'm a military man. Art
is not worth wasting time over
Here's three acres of
painting and carving by men
without the sense to take what's offered

Give an artist some fruit and wine
a naked courtesan on a couch
and he'll start fiddling with shade and texture
Meanwhile any man with common sense
will have eaten the fruit, gulped the wine
laid the woman and not wasted a yard of canvas
perfectly good for patching tents

Take this Rembrandt: there's hardly
enough light to show us what
he was missing,
while he painted away

but you, walking towards me
now there's art for the taking, the way
your long legs lead to two good handfuls of ass
a pretty little waist and long smooth arms
dark hair, full lips and fatal eyes
even an artist might notice
(though he'd knock over the easel
on the way to the couch)

all those painters aiming at Eve should see you

11

your walk that says Paradise is still here
I'll open those gates, girl, so your beauty
knocks the figures off their plinths
Truth, Justice, Honour, Virtue shattering

under the attack of honest lust
I'll describe the Tropics
and the dangers of my work
while I maneuver you onto that couch
We'll turn art back into life
or your hips are lying to me
and I know how to read hips."

How's that, Rudy? Wake up, you drunk.
Your little wife dramatized
your inmost thoughts
and you missed it. All right, I'm
coming to bed.

My Son as a New Island

No one knows all the islands of
the Java Sea. In this region
geography is no solid science
The earth's blood boils, a raw cone
pushes through steaming ocean.
Waves unfurl
like eyelids after a long sleep.

New island.
Soon vines snake over and fasten, orchids bloom
trees root to nothing known
birds discuss possibilities.

No one walks this shore that meets
the sea like a torn hem.
No map squared it with parallels
or announced a new name
to long for.

How soon this cycle reverses.
Sea's womb reopens
rock swims through the vanishing point
vines dive into watery declensions
of green. Astounded fish watch
an orchid plummet past.

And the unknown island is
one more wreck
in the ocean's lap, a word
murmured
for the sake of forgetting.

Fist of No

Meet the happy couple
domestic and useful.

I am slender, sharp and bright
and slammed into the floor
by this hammer of a husband.

His fist's a stuck telegraph key
that pounds out the same word
over and over NO.

Meinher Hammer likes things simple.
(A nail goes in straight
or wrong.) Sober or drunk,
obey him or disobey.

Attack or retreat, sex/sleep,
attention or at ease. All my
choices knocked down to his
while the gamelan orchestra
on the jasmine breeze plays the harmony
of a hundred other possibilities.

To him I am a jungle warp of curves
he must flatten into a cenotaph.
No to what my dreams suggest.
No to the beauty other men see.
No to anything but the weight of his will.

Husband, beware. The slender nail
sings long after it is hit
pierces the floor and is gone.
Without me you're an iron head
that has lost the only word it knows.

The Gamelan

After the screaming fight with my husband
I visit my other world
(he has only alcohol)
At the temple the gamelan orchestra plays
led by the old drummer, hands roughened
by rice-harvests and music
Other farmers play the gongs, the shrill flutes
This music is their true work
A certain melody must be played
once every seven years
or the heavens will not consent to revolve

This music forms and varies
time, fits within
generations improvising on the same theme
each long phrase marked
by the largest gong

I close my eyes. Notes become
meteorites falling, rain on the roof
tiny nails closing the coffin-lid of self

I start to dance, a tree swaying
among these small loin-clothed men
the gamelan counts and clangs
pauses, redoubles
until the morning light glows through me
One man breathes "she is Mata Hari"
and another agrees:
within this gamelan I am
the eye of dawn, the sun
magnified by morning mist

This music never stops. Players are replaced
the heavens hear their melody again
and consent once more to revolve

For one night my pulse
and the drums were the same
everything turned around me

Death is nothing, nor life either,
for that matter. To die, to sleep, to pass
into nothingness, what does it matter?
Everything is an illusion.

Typhoid Fever

Typhoid takes me
steam in the brain
lose touch with life
as we know it

explore elsewhere: reconnaissance
know it over or not at all
under the white sun of spring
sap boils out of treetops
forms a phantom tree

lose control
over me: mother wife invalid
I'm in-valid will never be
the same again
any sane agony

it hurts to change
knots of thunder in my joints
blood boils like stagnant water
when something rots underneath

shivers and stings and mal de mer
and mother's tears
for babies Pik and Jan Fluit

one's gone, poisoned for sins
of the elders, sick old story

the warm climes unhealthy
but soft (here under the pith helmet
diked by gun and culture and royal decree!
stern cold Dutch safe)

I'm a Frisian
with fever

don't resemble
any other

I must be a foundling
recessive gene they say
can't disguise the Jewish blood in me
can't hide the Javanese

she's not one of us
I'm not one of you

fairy child gone, boiled away
brain soup, cauliflower white sun
who am I in the great solvent
of sickness

fever child watching ballerinas dance
first position green on black
wallpaper, fevered swim
through sheets of sloughed-off skin
in monsoon
all the same no names here
you're a sick woman
I'm a sick woman, yes

don't drink don't breathe
speak only to natives
as if they were servants

my child, my son
black vomit over his face
"Mama, help me, help"
cure

something the father did
(fucked/killed/ordered

as soldier business)
my son, gone monsoon
rain washing everything off
the thatched roof, the palms

hand is destiny, mudras, mantras
the hand knows what to say
mine is hot
the lines writhe snakily

changing courses in mid-dream
new fevers of form, malcontent
sucking my force into its fog roots

brain on a string pegged to body
that fever strums storms, cloud

I'm cold, shower of sweat
something's prowling through tendrils and vine
a shadow weaving moiré patterns

an idea loose from the zoo of form
tiger/ Maya/ all is void
hunting me, meaning, moans

come awake breaking through skin of dream
and my husband's voice like a grater
"five guilders a day for the milk for her, five guilders a day"

no, I'm not worth it
pour the milk in
fat and chalk on my tongue
and it becomes fever cloud blood
on the horns of moon

fall back and let fever steam my brain

barely attached
stem to an out-of-whack watch
counting how long sick takes to strike
snakes crawling
up to my wrist
to wave their rattles for baby
who'll drop into sweet sleep

bailing out
fragile craft of my being
with a broken glass
in it the fever settles

from ashes I arise
at last I know who I'm not

Nightmare of the Dutch

These damned countrymen of mine
spout like dolphins about what is right
and proper, conventional, decent.
Scorn anything new, different
undefined.

The wall they raise of cheese
church, family to defend
their platoon of platitudes.

And the enemy?
I, as Dutch in my soul
as the Buddha, whisper it to you:
The Dutch stole this land field by field
from the sea. Staked it down
tied it up with dikes, polders, barns.
Stuck up windmills to scarecrow fish away.

Blink, and those Holsteins are schools of herring.
Blink, the immaculate farmhouse is a barnacled
grey whale.
Now you see it: the burghers are squid
the child with the sleek head, curious eye
belongs to the seals.

The Dutch really fear
that their virtue, work and prayer
will stand up as well as the borders of Poland
when Germany or Russia gets restive. One night
Neptune will call back his domain
march conquering waves over the land
so darkness again dances endlessly
with the undefined.

Debut at the Museé Guimet, Paris

My dance is a sacred poem in which each movement
is a word and whose every word is underlined by music
—Mata Hari to the audience, after the performance
in 1905 that launched her career.

Golden collar around my throat, pearls on my tawny
arms and legs
I stand in a fog of incense, incantation
from sitar and tabla
faces stuffed with Parisian food and money
goggling at me

I dance for the statue facing me, Shiva
in his aspect of King of Dancers
right foot crushing the dwarf of ignorance, left upraised
perfectly balanced with four arms above, face calm
halo of flame and emanations
scrolling from his ears

The truth of this dance animates me.
I take my past, my grief, marriage
my failure as wife, artist's model, circus rider,
my arrival in the City Of Light
a revolver and half a franc in my purse
nothing to trade but my body and brains

I crush all beneath my feet,
crush and re-create myself
strip the flesh and long dark hair
of Margaretha Gertruuida Zelle MacLeod from my bones
stamp her bones to dust and sweep it away with my hands
now birds, now flames, now invitations to sexual frenzy

The Parisians have never seen anything like this
They know someone is dying,
someone is being seduced
but aren't sure who

This drama is older than Paris
whose centuries are one posture in Shiva's dance
whose Opera and sieges and guillotines
mere symptoms of his music and fire

scouring human dirt from the planet
until the metal at the centre shines through

I offer my life through my body
to my lord of creation destruction
and bear a new woman through jewelled loins.
Afterward I tell the crowd the old story of Shiva in French
then in English, German, Dutch, Javanese.
They know to join my dance is to forget themselves
My final gesture seduces each of them
into the abyss of mystery

Each feels a shiver that starts at the genitals
and runs straight up the spine
sparking the urge to say

Fuck the family, fuck the past, civilization,
my tiresome self
junk the lot and start afresh.

Care to dance?

Kama Sutra

Men provide courtesans with two satisfactions: sexual fulfillment and pleasure, and the means of earning a livelihood. When a courtesan proposes to give herself to a man she loves, this action is natural; but when she submits to him only to earn money the action is forced and artificial. However, even in the second circumstance she should behave as if she loved him, because men prefer women who are devoted and attentive to them.
— from Vatsyayana's *Kama Sutra*

Wise Vatsyayana, the von Clausewitz of love!
Any woman could profit from this wonderful book
which assumes that sexual pleasure
should be sought by both sexes
that a woman grows richer in soul from
learning the arts of love
and shame and guilt should arise only
when orgasm is pursued at the expense
of spiritual and material progress

Seduction, adultery and manipulating others' desires
are all permissible tactics
Every stage and act of love is defined
and given its proper place
Against the logic of this Hindu sage
convention does not hold, morality weakens, even
the Commandments seem uncertain

To the fulminating pastors of Europe
who denounce their own desires
as the work of Satan every Sunday
I give the eight kinds of pressure with fingers:
Line
Circle
Sonorous
Half Moon

The Tiger's Claw
The Peacock's Claw
The Leap of the Hare
The Leap of the Blue Lotus

To the gossiping housewives of Holland
who wring others' affairs out like laundry
but (Heavens! The very idea) never sin
I utter the eight sounds
of pleasurable anguish:
Hinn
Phoutt
Phatt
Soutt
Platt
A Tonal Sound
a Cooing Sound
a Crying Sound

To the mustached husbands of the colonial army
who in the name of honour
keep closed the thighs of their wives
while trying to unlock
those of all other women
I mark you with:
the Hidden Bite
the Swollen Bite
the Point
the Line of Points
the Coral and the Jewel
the Line of Jewels
the Broken Cloud
the Bite of the Wild Boar

And to men everywhere who believe
women are to be won, used, discarded

I offer a challenge:
with my beauty and these teachings
in any game I hold the better hand
because Vatsyayana shows
the clever courtesan never
approaches a man directly
but uses his vanity and self-love to win her ends

If I desire gifts, I'll first
praise your intelligence
If desire for me wanes
I'll flirt with other men and use special ointments
to make you ache for me
until you must have me back
and when I tire of you
I will recall this verse:
"Always she will ask him
For things he cannot give her"

and when I leave, I will turn
and favour you
with one last quotation:

"The dimensions of women's love are fathomless
Even the beloved cannot sound its depths:
For the subtlety, delicacy and natural restraint
Veils the image of love in mystery.
Women can never be seen in the light of their pure nature,
Whether they love or are indifferent,
Whether they satisfy or turn away in distaste,
Not even when they succeed in grasping
All the fortune a man possesses."

Salomé

In 1911, after a long pursuit of the role, Mata Hari danced
the part of Salomé at the Palazzo Barberini. The opera by
Richard Strauss was inspired by Oscar Wilde's writing,
considered the height of decadence.

What Carmen hints at, this opera shrieks.
Women murder as well as they conceive
with all powers of mistress
mother, femme fatale

Kali, consort of Shiva, incarnates seduction
yet human skulls form her necklace
She dances on the corpse heap of
men she's killed
before she consumes them

The praying mantis eats her mate
as dessert during copulation
She who gives life takes it back
This opera states a truth
that convention denies
I was born to dance this role
my mastery of men a rehearsal

Herod wants her body, slowly revealed
Salomé the head of that prophet
so inflated with futile holiness
that it floated away from her beauty
towards God

Offered anything to dance
all she will reply is "the head of Iokannon"

Now only virgins are holy
Christians mortify their flesh, fast
call sex a ruse of Satan

When I dance Salomé I'll take their heads off
while the music cracks and thumps
like a soul forced back into flesh

My body the revelation, the fruit, the truth
my arms become swords, my thighs crack bones
eyes the windows of an ancient temple
stippling a sacrifice with honeyed light
I strip off the veils
until my body gleams through

The king groans, comes on his throne
and the prophet's head shoots from his neck
because he finally remembers what a woman is:
the chalice of life, death, the newly born

I ravish the audience and withdraw
they applaud, cannot look at each other
I have remade sex holy
my body ringing doom like a gong
a sound they'll not hear again
until someone dances them away
for good

Figurehead Dream

A buxom wooden woman
painted in bright polychrome
I cut waves at a good clip
as wind flutes through my chiseled hair
water foams over my polished waist
"She's got a bone in her teeth," old sailors said
watching a clipper split the sea like this

Ships are "she" because their figureheads
breast the water and men
try to make them obey
with ropes and knots and wise old saws
I'm a figurehead who's quit her ship
My lips fix a grin
Men don't want complexities

Bone in my teeth
figure of speech caught in my head
tongue sealed by salt wind

Grey destroyers hunt me
massive bows curved like absolute physics
fade into mist as they taper behind
They arc and skid on the sea
trying to split my wood with their metal
pass through each other like ghosts

I aim my brushed-on smile at the future
My wake a wedge of bubbling surf
that ships bisect and bury
They close on me as the sun
rises and paints the ocean with fire

I catch and torch into an icon
The destroyers dull to fillets of spent force

Steaming water streams behind me
like a bridal veil
I ascend the column of my burning
Figurehead to the sky

Interview with a Journalist

How can I entrap any man, you ask?

At first just listen, observe.
Say little but keep a subtle smile on your lips.
He will not know whether you are mocking
or his attentions please you.
Ask who he is, what he wants.
Say little about yourself
until you find the way in.

When you look in the mirror, who
is there?
See the being the world perceives.
Alter that person,
be who he imagines.

If he wants a mother,
soothe and caress.
Give the breast men were denied long ago.
Give suckle.
Murmur endearments when he tells you
how little he is appreciated. When he balks
at buying gifts, deny him.
He will return.

If he professes to be the great lover,
the superman who pleasures any woman,
be shy. Pretend that
you have never had a true jouissance. Show him
only the most conventional ways of lovemaking.
Be modest in the bedroom, close your
eyes at the sight of engorgement.
Become that creature
who lives for his embrace.
Moan "You have awoken me!"

For those who believe, for all their power,
they deserve to be punished,
cannot stay hard without pain and scorn,
be stern. You are that shapely teacher
they desired but never deserved,
the bitch-goddess with
quick hand. Each sting is to them
an encouragement to gallop.

You see the game. Learn what he wants,
metamorphose into that.
You have hooked your trout.

Remember Blake:
"What is it that men in women do require?
The lineaments of gratified desire."

Madrid Tango

Palace Hotel, Madrid, New Year's Eve, 1916

The tango is perfect seduction
a warm breeze from the shores of Argentina
the perfect dance for all double agents here
we glide across the floor in pairs
feet moving smoothly as snake ribs

I hardly know who holds my hand
he is slender and proud
and does not know all that I am
in the addiction of tango
we drop our masks

I am not unproductive Agent H21
ex-performer aging charmer
I am pure feminine essence
silken as my gown
he is only a man
the music's magnet forms our elements
two straight lines that cross the floor
reverse, fall back in 2/4 time

this dance is brandy in veins
flamenco slowed by South American sun

we pass the blonde French woman
who whispers to my chambermaid
held by Prince Ratibor, the new German ambassador
there the little man who shadowed me
behind potted palms in the Paris Hotel
forgets suspicion as he stares
into the eyes of a Portuguese agent

any woman could become a spy
she already knows the first rule:

never show the enemy what you really want
wear the mask he finds most pleasing

I have been dancer, courtesan, spy
but like Shiva I destroy
as my quick feet create
tonight I'm that woman
who never let the past lead her steps

and you, holding me, are any man
from a dozen nations, allied, neutral, pro-German
what you want from me tonight
is not information,
gratification or applause
but a body that knows where you'll turn
before you do
a back that sings like a violin in your hand
an elegant arm that stretches as far as yours

so we turn and pace and dip

at midnight all kiss, and champagne corks
salute like the artillery a few hundred miles away
Noisemakers blow out, tongues of the dead
a new year begins for this weary war

I've had enough of suspecting
and suspicion in return
the cure for my malaise is more tango
across the curling ribbons of crepe
squashed funny hats and broken glasses

I'll trade any secret for one more dance
and you'll destroy your career
for me   aging and ageless

beautiful and sad, sore feet, a hangover
but my eyes reflect the dawn

although the morning dispels the party like fog
part of me is dancing still
among the snoring spies and empty bottles
masks and mirrors of the Palace Hotel
with a shadow that favours
all the men who wanted me

Making Up

(to my maid, Anna Lintjens)

Hand me the mascara, Anna
Eyes were always my best offence
I must be getting old, or vulnerable

Remember I said, to enjoy men
you must not fall in love?
The man you loved left you pregnant
among the clucking tongues of Holland
The man I loved drank and beat me
and got our son poisoned

After that I made my armour
from pearls and smiles and caresses
No man would breach my heart again
We'd have a fair exchange: my body and skill
for his body and wealth

Never let them see you smile
the man who makes you smile thinks
he can make you do anything
The sadness I locked in my eyes
made even nobles feel small

You like my hair up like this?
The lines beside my eyes don't show too much?
For years it worked. Even that banker
who kept me in style at the Villa Rémy
had me, but not my soul

But this boy, Vadim
brave enough to fly
in the laughable Russian air force
undid my chain mail because he needs me
I want him beside me now

I weep for each wound he suffers
I'm a foolish old woman, Anna

But I believe in art
especially the art of make-up
Now I look ten years younger
I might make men believe again
I'm Mata Hari
I'll go out tonight
best them once more
to buy one more weekend with Vadim
Then you can put me in a box
and send me back to Leuuwarden. Tell them
the stone over my head should say
"She had the last laugh
by dying for love."

*I have encountered in this world
riff-raff and good people. I lose. I win.
I defend myself when I am attacked.
I take when someone has taken from me.
But I beg you to believe me;
I have never done an act of espionage
against France. Never. Never.*

Trial by Tongues: Paris, July 1917

As for myself, I have been sincere. My life and my self-
interest are the guarantee of that. Today, around me,
everything is collapsing, everyone turns his back, even he
for whom I would have gone through fire. Never would I
have believed in so much human cowardice. Well, so be it.
I am alone. I will defend myself and if I must fall it will be
with a smile of profound contempt.
— Mata Hari, in a letter written a month before her trial

We all know what's to happen here
why bother going through formalities?
The jurors are to answer
whether I betrayed France in eight different ways
one yes is excuse enough
for a firing squad to perform its little pas de feux

The prosecution weaves French inflections
into a shimmering web. As in espionage
language must be opaque
nothing meaning what it says
much like modern poetry
where a speeding car means a woman
who stands for time

The Germans sent a telegram in code
they knew the French could interpret
in it the code for me

The spectators appreciate my fine French
my lucidity, my verve, but the jury's ears
open only for the accent of French honour
bruised and skinned by this unwinnable war

It must be my fault, I am here, notorious
the government needs good press
my lovers and patrons will not speak here

my own words are turned against me
they try to prove my contraceptive cream
is a clever disguise for secret ink

Verbs strip me, adjectives lash and cut
red-hot nouns brand my prison-dull skin
loaded phrases tighten around my neck

I who speak five languages, love poetry,
played Salomé, whose hips
could take off a prophet's head

Although I defend myself well, my old fool
lawyer stammers and splutters, archaic footnotes
tack his tongue to his palate

Language is how we handle the world
yet its wrappings conceal reality
the art of Maya
is to name, call out, denounce

I hear the feet of the dancer whose steps destroy
even in this military court
where the prosecution's logical cannon besiege me
in the cadences and rhetorical flourishes
fired beneath French mustaches

My work for the Germans
killed 50,000 Allied soldiers, they say
Let us then apportion the blame:
10,000 corpses for each melancholy dark eye
whole regiments for each shapely knee
a division swept aside by my elegant arms
(the most beautiful in the world, an admirer said)
but all the rest rot in a trench
dug and mined by my lying tongue

that said one thing
clearly meaning, the prosecution shows, another
I was a counterspy, double meaning
une agente horizontale, hotel bed my campaign field

back in my cell I was in good company
two decades ago Madame Steinhel stayed here
whose tongue so delighted the President of France
his heart stopped as he clutched her curly head
to his loins. He died happier
than this grim jury will ever be

but my mind wanders
they prepare the verdict, the sentence
"I must die" the message concealed
under this interminable cypher of a trial

Last Conversation with the Prison Nun

Sister, do you know the real reason
the French condemn me to death?
Nothing to do with waltzing
with German naval attachés, visiting
French aerodromes, or selling
secrets half of Europe already knew
Nor with
the prosecution's Cartesian arguments
"evidence," "logic," even my outrageous
reputation. Nothing, Sister.

The reason is male aesthetics. My beauty
Medusaed so many men. How they loved to
stiffen under my dark eyes.
Cabinet ministers and police chiefs lined up.
But the moment my looks began to leave
some called a strategic retreat.
Others attacked.

I have known so many men
in a way you have known none. But even you
must have seen that weakness in strong men
when something they love fades.
That is why generals who campaigned
with bouquets champagne and diamonds
to win one night with me
have deserted. Soon
they'll be their future:
mediocre statues abandoned in parks, targets
only for pigeons and bitter veterans who
recall their vanity and foolishness.

I have read, Sister, of the Japanese
samurai. Without a thought, believing himself
already dead, he would behead a peasant for
an insufficiently low bow

or launch himself alone at 100 enemies
without fear. Yet the same man
would prize a single
trampled flower, and compose
a poem for it.

In my declining looks, the French scent
their own death.
My crime is treason against allure:
having so much
then losing it.
The instant they catch
their wives having an affair with time
they move to younger mistresses.

No such domestic arrangements
for this Scarlet Dancer. Just a final
penetration from 12 bullets
— an act not of justice, war, or love
only a critique.

Incandescence

Sun on the mountains turned
to storm and what went
through us could have been anything
in its instant —
rock turned to cloud
the Greek alphabet in newness

but the lightning took
a tree instead of us
and we escaped, scared normal humans
before a second stroke made us
saints and cinders

does any lightning bring me
back on your line
the way it snaps stills for me
of you on the rocks that day?

Ghost

An alteration of the air at the Villa Rémy
shadows dappling a bay horse seem
to rise and turn into a woman riding

wind's robe whirls around a node where dust
and leaves spin for the forest mistress
a garment of shadowed trails and pools of light
vestments of loss, dancing around no body

when the wine is gone a different bouquet remains
air taking on lightness
such is my ghost: the world, mother of all
cannot stand to lose all her children
to the bullet or microbe
so she keeps our most volatile essences
to flavour the world
after the wine is drunk, bottle smashed

in the garage's sad darkness
where Daimlers
and Peugeots purred for my guests
the signal of my eyes still flashes

on the steps where I posed, a statue of desire
carved by the gaze of wealthy men
my absence forms a longing the visitor cannot place

these images hold as much truth as the other
tales about my execution:

that at the command to fire I threw off my fur coat
my nakedness so dazzled the 12 Zouaves
they shot two larks and ten paths of air
and I escaped
to live out my old age

or it was a publicity ploy
morale-building for a war-tired public
with blanks in the guns and after the performance –
I died so bravely, slowly crumpling in the gun smoke –
champagne and kisses as usual in a limousine
(this last unlikely because so few adults have
the courage to enter a fairy tale)

I prefer this: I spun on dancer's soles
like a dervish, boring down
through the earth as rifles spat above
I swam through earth's boiling heart and
came up through a Java volcano where
I am worshipped by natives
fanning me with palm fronds
and advise young girls on
how to love and not lose

or I am Hari's comet crossing the skies
whenever a great man is disgraced by lust
although I never brought anyone down —
our fall sleeps within us
until our own acts make it real

we need ghosts because facts are so brutally dull
I was shot through the heart, my face blown off
with a .45 calibre coup de grace
and the body that Europe once worshipped
carted to medical students for dissection

that is only the body's truth

the spirit that made me dance
rides that horse through shifting shadows
in a forest afternoon forever

*The temple in which I dance
can be vague or faithfully reproduced,
for I am the temple*

Mata - Hari

John Oughton was born in Guelph, Ontario, a block away from the home of John McCrae (author of *"In Flanders Fields"*). When his father was seconded to the World Health Organization, John spent two years living in Egypt and Iraq. He completed a BA and MA in English at York University, where he studied with Irving Layton, Eli Mandel, Miriam Waddington and Frank Davey.

After a half-year stay in Kyoto, Japan, he worked at Coach House Press and as a journalist and corporate communicator. He attended the Jack Kerouac School of Disembodied Poetics at Naropa University, and was a research assistant to Allen Ginsberg and Anne Waldman.

John taught English, led faculty development, and recently retired as Professor of Learning and Teaching, at Centennial College, Ontario. He now free-lances as an editor, including of poetry manuscripts, and writer. Visit his website: JOughton.Wixsite.com/author.

In 2015, he published an acclaimed, offbeat mystery novel about the Kennedy assassination, *Death by Triangulation* (NeoPoiesis Press). Oughton has also penned five books of poetry, most recently *Time Slip* (Guernica Editions), and over 400 articles, interviews, reviews and blogs. John is a long-time member of the Long Dash writing workshop.

He is an accomplished photographer with three solo shows and several book and magazine covers to his credit. For fun, he plays guitar and drums. He rides an old Yamaha motorcycle.

John Oughton – Publications

Taking Tree Trains
Coach House Press, Toronto, 1973

Gearing of Love
Mosaic Press, Oakville, 1984

rImbAud'S twISted baLLS (Chapbook)
Two Bit Editions, Toronto, 1986

Mata Hari's Lost Words
Ragweed Press, Charlottetown, PEI, 1988

Counting Out the Millennium
Pecan Grove Press, San Antonio, Texas, 1997

***A little endarkenment and in my poetry you find me:
the Naropa Institute interview with Robert Duncan***,
with Anne Waldman. Rodent Press, Boulder, CO, 1997

You Can't Win (Chapbook)
Interview of William Burroughs with Anne Waldman
Elik Press, Salt Lake City, 2001

Take With You What You've Left (Chapbook)
Sixth Floor Press, Toronto, 2003

Time Slip: New and Selected Poems
Guernica Editions, Toronto, 2010

Death by Triangulation
Neopoiesis Press, Seattle, 2015

Vertex/Vertigo (Chapbook)
Big Pond Rumours Press, Sarnia, ON, 2016

NeoPoiesis: *a new way of making*

1) in ancient Greece, poiesis referred to the process of making: creation - production - organization - formation - causation

2) a process that can be physical and spiritual, biological and intellectual, artistic and technological, material and teleological, efficient and formal

3) a means of modifying the environment and a method of organizing the self, the making of art and music and poetry, the fashioning of memory and history and philosophy, the construction of perception and expression and reality

4) an independent publisher with a steadfast goal to print and promote outstanding poets, writers and artists who reflect the creative drive and spirit of the new electronic landscape

NeoPoiesisPress.com